DISCOVER 🐾 DOGS WITH
THE AMERICAN CANINE ASSOCIATION

I LIKE
BULLDOGS!

Linda Bozzo

It is the Mission of the American Canine Association (ACA) to provide registered dog owners with the educational support needed for raising, training, showing, and breeding the healthiest pets expected by responsible pet owners throughout the world. Through our activities and services, we encourage and support the dog world in order to promote best-known husbandry standards as well as to ensure that the voice and needs of our customers are quickly and properly addressed.

Our continued support, commitment, and direction are guided by our customers, including veterinary, legal, and legislative advisors. ACA aims to provide the most efficient, cooperative, and courteous service to our customers and strives to set the standard for education and problem solving for all who depend on our services.

For more information, please visit www.acacanines.com, e-mail customerservice@acadogs.com, phone 1-800-651-8332, or write to the American Canine Association at PO Box 121107, Clermont, FL 34712.

Published in 2017 by Enslow Publishing, LLC.
101 W. 23rd Street, Suite 240, New York, NY 10011

Copyright © 2017 by Enslow Publishing, LLC.

All rights reserved.

No part of this book may be reproduced by any means without the written permission of the publisher.

Library of Congress Cataloging-in-Publication Data
Names: Bozzo, Linda.
Title: I like bulldogs! / Linda Bozzo.
Description: New York, NY : Enslow Publishing, 2017. | Series: Discover dogs with the American Canine Association | Includes bibliographical references and index. | Audience: Ages 5 and up. | Audience: Grades K to 3.
Identifiers: LCCN 2015044487 | ISBN 9780766079205 (library bound) | ISBN 9780766077911 (pbk.) | ISBN 9780766077638 (6-pack)
Subjects: LCSH: Bulldog--Juvenile literature.
Classification: LCC SF429.B85 B69 2017 | DDC 636.72--dc23
LC record available at http://lccn.loc.gov/2015044487

Printed in Malaysia

To Our Readers: We have done our best to make sure all website addresses in this book were active and appropriate when we went to press. However, the author and the publisher have no control over and assume no liability for the material available on those websites or on any websites they may link to. Any comments or suggestions can be sent by e-mail to customerservice@enslow.com.

Photo Credits: Cover, p. 1 WilleeCole Photography/Shutterstock.com; pp. 3, 4 Victoria Rak/Shutterstock.com; p. 5 Sattahipbeach/Shutterstock.com; p. 6 Dien/Shutterstock.com; p. 7 Grisha Bruev/Shutterstock.com; p. 9 Carol Yates/Moment/Getty Images; p. 10 Milan Stojanovic/Shutterstock.com; p. 13 Tatiana Katsai/Shutterstock.com; p. 13 jclegg/shutterstock.com (collar), Luisa Leal Photography (bed), gvictoria/Shutterstock.com (brush), In-Finity/Shutterstock.com (dishes), Lisa Thornberg/iStock (leash, toys); p. 14 Ron Chappie Stock/Thinkstock; p. 15 Tannis Toohey/Toronto Star/Getty Images; p. 16 Annette Shaff/Shutterstock.com; p. 17 LWA/Dann Tardiff/Blend Images/Getty Images; p. 18 Belinda Images/Belinga Images/SuperStock; p. 19 Jamie Squire/Getty Images Sport; p. 21 GK Hart/Vikki Hart/Stokebyte/Getty Images; p. 22 Rita Kochmarjova/Shutterstock.com.

Enslow Publishing
101 W. 23rd Street
Suite 240
New York, NY 10011
USA
enslow.com

TINLEY PARK PUBLIC LIBRARY

CONTENTS

IS A BULLDOG RIGHT FOR YOU? 4

A DOG OR A PUPPY? 7

LOVING YOUR BULLDOG 8

EXERCISE 11

FEEDING YOUR BULLDOG 12

GROOMING 15

WHAT YOU SHOULD KNOW 16

A GOOD FRIEND 19

NOTE TO PARENTS 20

WORDS TO KNOW 22

READ ABOUT DOGS (BOOKS AND WEBSITES) 23

INDEX 24

IS A BULLDOG RIGHT FOR YOU?

Bulldogs are friendly and make great family pets. They get along with other pets by ignoring them. Bulldogs can be lazy. They are not the best choice for very active families.

Bulldogs are not very active indoors. They are good dogs if you live in an apartment.

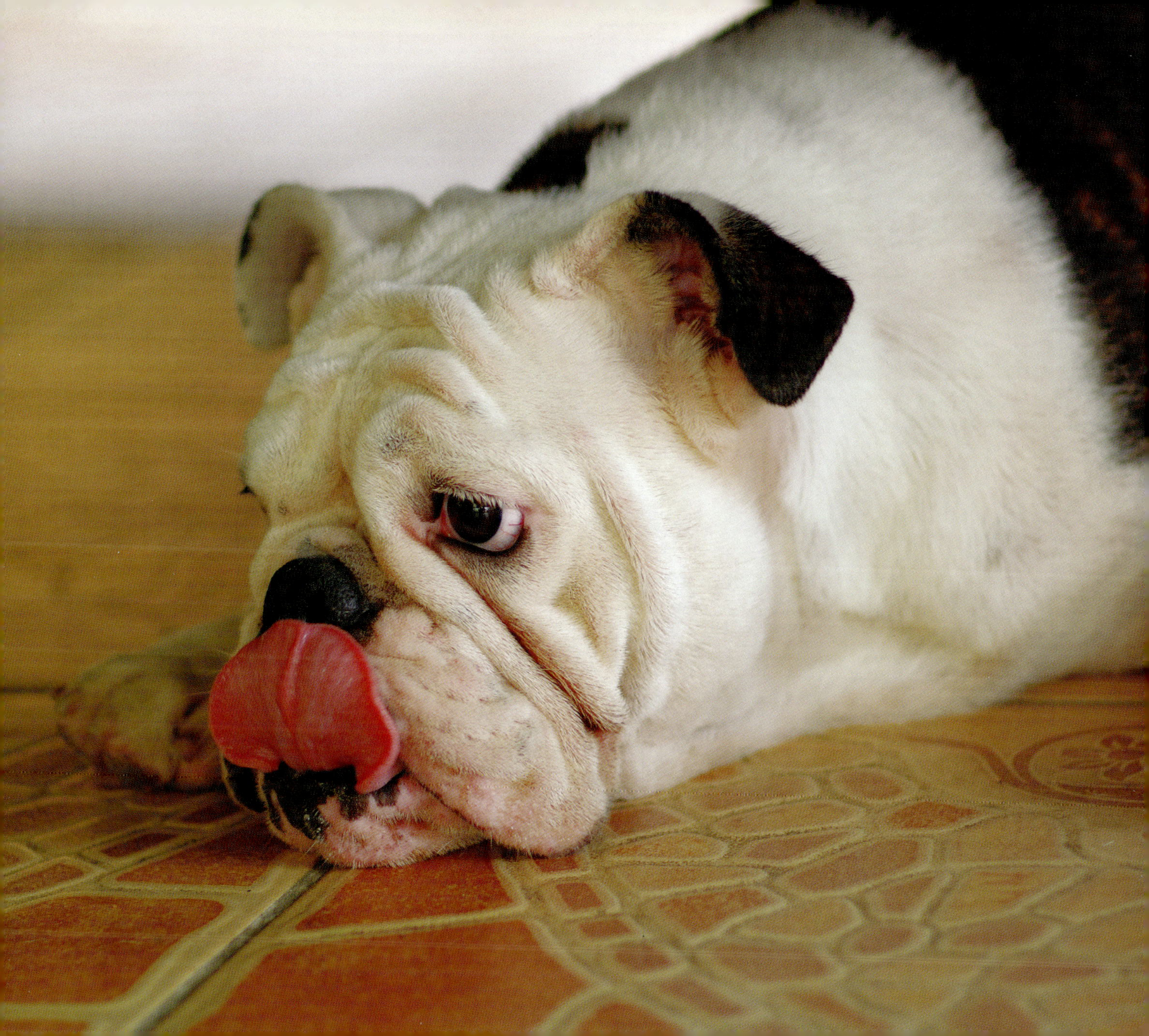

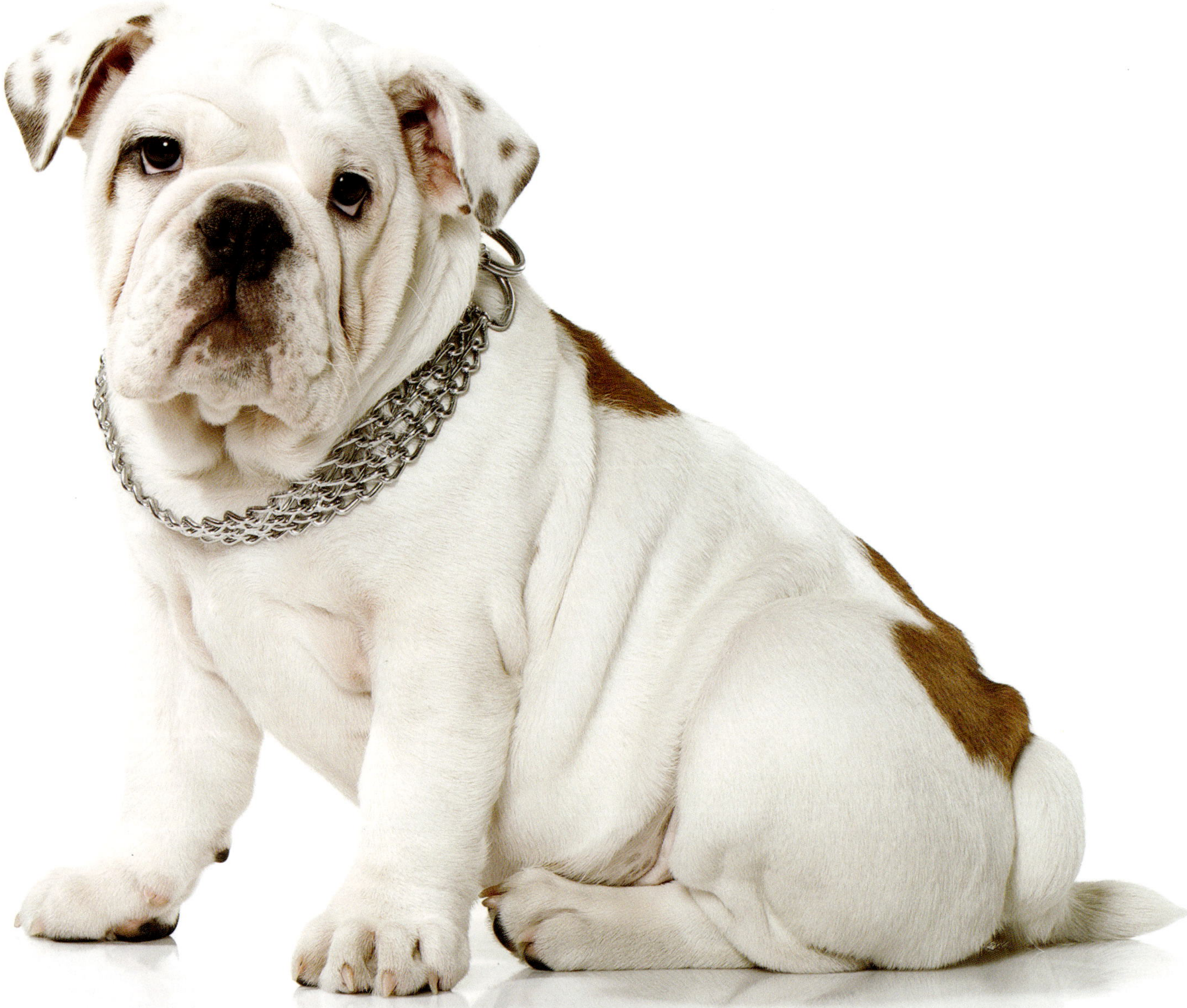

A DOG OR A PUPPY?

Bulldog puppies, with their wrinkled faces, are cute. But they can be **stubborn**, so training a puppy could take some time. If you do not have time to train a puppy, your family may want to get an older dog.

Bulldogs grow to be medium in size, 45-55 lbs (20-25 kg).

LOVING YOUR BULLDOG

Your bulldog will love to run and jump. He will also like to snore and sleep after a good romp. Bulldogs may look tough, but they are easy to love!

Show your bulldog love, and he will love you right back!

🐾
Your dog will like a shady spot to rest.

EXERCISE

Bulldogs have short legs that hold up their big bodies. Walks with your bulldog on a **leash** should be slow and kept short. Bulldogs don't like the heat, so it's best not to walk them in the heat of the day.

FEEDING YOUR BULLDOG

Bulldogs need a careful diet to keep trim. Dogs can be fed wet or dry dog food. Ask a **veterinarian** (vet), a doctor for animals, which food is best for your bulldog and how much to feed her.

Give your bulldog fresh, clean water every day.

Remember to keep your dog's food and water dishes clean. Dirty dishes can make a dog sick.

Do not feed your dog people food.
It can make her sick.

Your new dog will need:

a collar with a tag

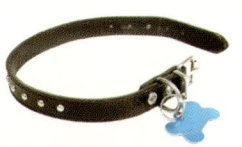

a bed

a brush

food and water dishes

a leash

toys

Food and dirt can get trapped in a bulldog's wrinkles. Keep dog wipes handy to clean them.

GROOMING

Bulldogs have a short smooth coat and **shed** a lot. This means their hair falls out often. Bulldogs should be brushed at least once a week. A bulldog's face wrinkles need to be cleaned regularly.

Your bulldog will need a bath every so often. A bulldog's nails need to be clipped. A vet or **groomer** can show you how. Your dog's ears should be cleaned. His teeth should be brushed by an adult.

FAST FACT: Use a gentle soap made just for dogs.

WHAT YOU SHOULD KNOW

A bulldog's short legs make walking up large stairs hard. They do not do well in very hot or very cold weather. Bulldogs have many health issues. You need to have the time and money to care for the health of a bulldog.

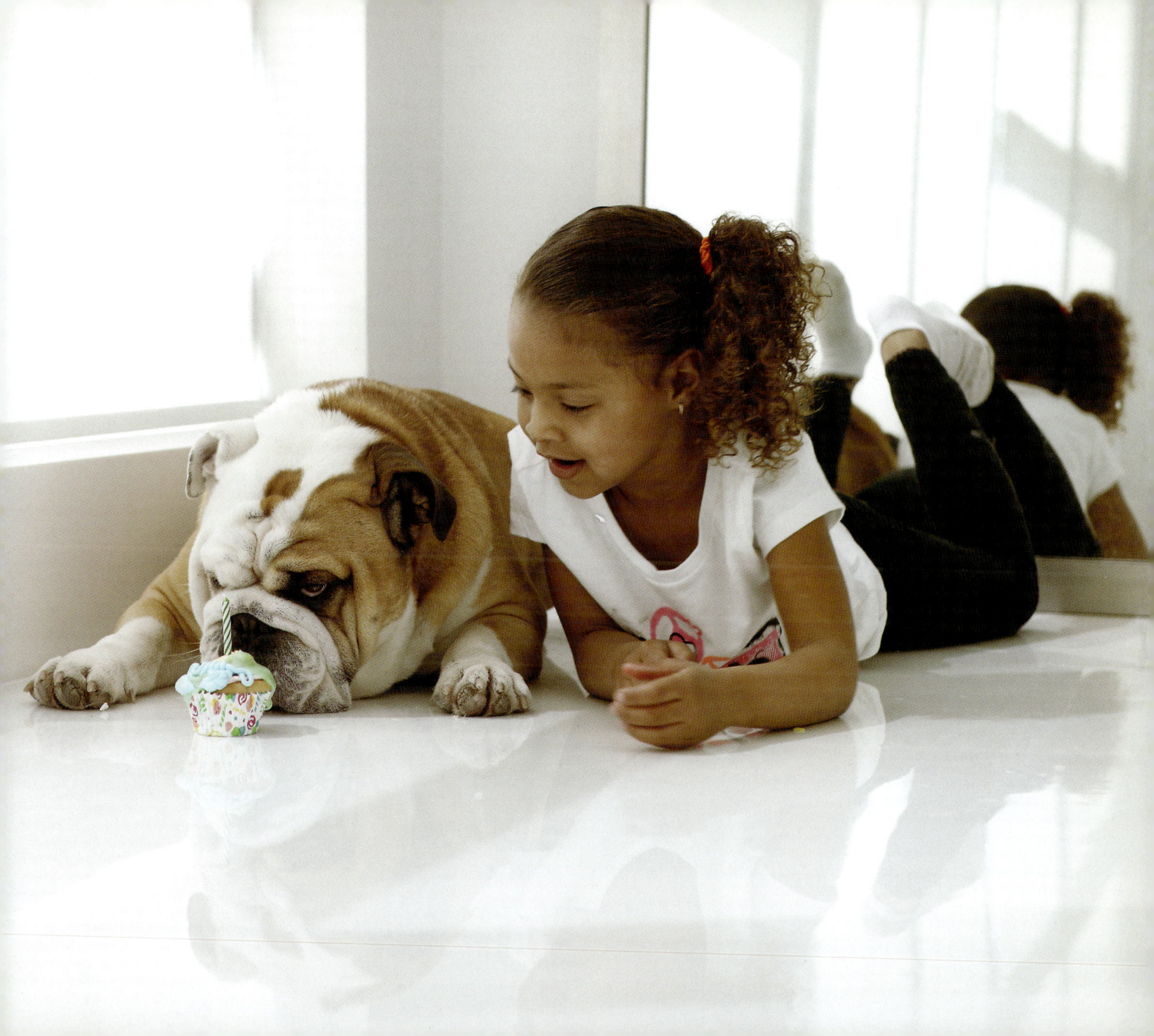

You will need to take your new dog to the vet for a checkup. He will need shots, called **vaccinations**, and yearly checkups to keep him healthy. If you think your dog may be sick, call your vet.

A GOOD FRIEND

With proper care, bulldogs can live up to 10 years. Like a good friend, they are fun and kind. Take care of her and your bulldog will bring you years of friendship.

FUN FACT: The bulldog is a common mascot for sports teams.

NOTE TO PARENTS

It is important to consider having your dog spayed or neutered when the dog is young. Spaying and neutering are operations that prevent unwanted puppies and can help improve the overall health of your dog.

It is also a good idea to microchip your dog, in case he or she gets lost. A vet will implant a painless microchip under the skin, which can then be scanned at a vet's office or animal shelter to look up your information on a national database.

Some towns require licenses for dogs, so be sure to check with your town clerk.

For more information, speak with a vet.

There are many dogs, young and old, waiting to be adopted from animal shelters and rescue groups.

21

Words to Know

groomer – A person who bathes and brushes dogs.

leash – A chain or strap that attaches to the dog's collar.

shed – When dog hair falls out so new hair can grow.

stubborn – Strong-willed and hard to handle.

vaccinations – Shots that dogs need to stay healthy.

veterinarian (vet) – A doctor for animals.

Read About Dogs

Books

Barnes, Nico. *Bulldogs*. Minneapolis, MN: Abdo Kids, 2014.

Bodden, Valerie. *Bulldogs*. Mankato, MN: Creative Education, 2014.

Johnson, Jinny. *Bulldog*. Mankato, MN: Smart Apple Media, 2013.

Websites

American Canine Association Inc., Kids Corner
acakids.com/

National Geographic for Kids, Pet Central
kids.nationalgeographic.com/explore/pet-central/

PBS Kids, Dog Games
pbskids.org/games/dog/

INDEX

A
activity level of bulldogs, 4
animal shelters, 20, 21

B
bathing, 15
beds for dogs, 13
body type of bulldogs, 11, 16
brushing, 13, 15

C
collars for dogs, 10, 13

D
dishes for dogs, 12, 13

E
exercise, 11

F
feeding, 12, 13

G
grooming, 15

H
health of bulldogs, 16

I
items needed for dogs, 13

L
leashes, 11, 13
licenses for dogs, 20
lifespan of bulldogs, 19

M
mascots, 19
microchips, 20

N
nail clipping, 15

O
other dogs and bulldogs, 4

P
personality of bulldogs, 4, 7, 16
puppies, 7, 20

S
size of bulldogs, 7
spaying/neutering, 20

T
tags for dogs, 13
toys for dogs, 13
training, 7

V
vaccinations, 18
veterinarians, 12, 15, 18, 20

W
walks, 11
water, 12, 13
weather needed for bulldogs, 11, 16
wrinkles of bulldogs, 7, 14, 15